I0006416

Vidita Sharma

Effective Decision Tree Algorithm For Reality Mining

K. Rameshkumar
Vidita Sharma

Effective Decision Tree Algorithm For Reality Mining

LAP LAMBERT Academic Publishing

Cover image: www.ingimage.com

Publisher:
LAP LAMBERT Academic Publishing
is a trademark of
International Book Market Service Ltd., member of OmniScriptum Publishing Group
17 Meldrum Street, Beau Bassin 71504, Mauritius

ISBN: 978-3-659-51627-6

Zugl. / Approved by: Chennai, Hindustan University, Diss., 2013

EFFECTIVE DECISION TREE ALGORITHM FOR REALITY MINING

DR. K. RAMESHKUMAR

ASSOCIATE PROFESSOR

HINDUSTAN UNIVERSITY

CHENNAI, INDIA

VIDITA SHARMA

HINDUSTAN UNIVERSITY

CHENNAI, INDIA

ACKNOWLEDGEMENT

We express my deep sense of gratitude to our Chancellor **Dr. Elizebeth Varghese,** Pro Chancellor **Dr.Anand Jacob Varghese,** Director **Mr.Ashok Varghese,** and Vice-Chancellor **Dr.S.Ramachandran**, who provided all facilities and encouragement during the course study. I humbly thank the Management of Hindustan University for their valuable facilitation for the lab facility provided.

We thank **Dr.S.Nagarajan**, Head of the Department and teaching and non-teaching staffs, Department of Information Technology, Hindustan University, whose encouragement was a great source of inspiration.

We dedicate this book to our family members

CONTENTS

1. INTRODUCTION

2. LITERATURE SURVEY

LIST OF ABBREVIATIONS

ID3	Iterative Dictomizer 3
ARCS	Association Rule Clustering System
CAEP	Classification by Aggregating Emerging Patterns
CBR	Case-Based Reasoning
kNN	K-nearest neighbor
CART	Classification and Regression Tree
KDD	Knowledge Data Discovery

LIST OF FIGURES

LIST OF TABLES

ABSTRACT

This project work deals with reality mining and decision tree. Reality mining is the collection and analysis of data where human social behavior is analyzed through machine-sensed environment, with the goal of identifying predictable patterns of behavior. Reality mining studies human interactions based on the usage of wireless devices such as mobile phones and GPS systems providing a more accurate picture of what people do, where they go, and with whom they communicate. This is important to understand the data which we are going to collect.

The data will be in the following manner:-

Communication Log: (date, text/call, incoming/outgoing, duration, number)
Phone Status: (charging, idle/active, current application in use)

Proximate (Visible) Bluetooth Devices: (date, mac, [device name] ...)
Celltower ID: (date, area, cell, network)
User-Defined Celltower Names: (area, cell, network, name)

Classification is the process of finding a model that describe and distinguishes data classes, with the purpose of using model to predict the class of objects whose class label is unknown. A decision tree is a decision support tool that uses a tree-like graph or model of decisions and their possible consequences, including chance event outcomes, resource costs, and utility. It is one way to display an algorithm. ID3 is mathematical algorithm for building the decision tree. It builds the tree from the top down recursive divide-and-conquer manner, with no backtracking. Advantages of ID3 are it build fast and short tree. Disadvantage is data may be over fitted and over classified if a small sample is tested. Only one attribute at a time is tested for making decision.

This project work:-

o   To study the drawback of existing decision tree algorithms.
o   To construct decision tree technique using R software.
o   To compare the decision tree with R using existing implementation.
o   To apply and study the decision tree with reality mining.

1.1 Introduction

Knowledge data discovery is very essential process in the field of decision making. Data mining is one of the well known techniques to extract knowledge from database. This chapter consists of the basic concepts of data mining, reality mining, classification and it will also specify the objective of project clearly. Currently reality mining although still in its infancy, but very soon it will be more common. In this chapter we discuss about all the above mention terms.

1.2 KDD

Many people treat data mining as a synonym for another popularly used term, Knowledge Discovery from Data, or KDD. Alternatively, others view data mining as simply an essential step in the process of knowledge discovery [10].

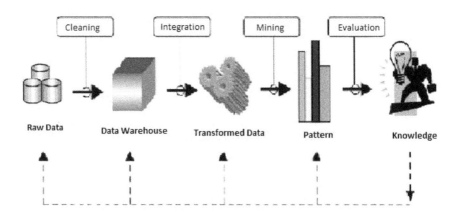

Figure 1.1 Knowledge Data Discovery Process

Knowledge discovery as a process is depicted in Figure and consists of an iterative sequence of the following steps:

1. Data cleaning to remove noise and inconsistent data.

2. Data integration where multiple data sources may be combined.

3. Data selection where data relevant to the analysis task are retrieved from the database.

4. Data transformation where data are transformed or consolidated into forms appropriate for mining by performing summary or aggregation operations, for instance.

5. Data mining an essential process where intelligent methods are applied in order to extract data patterns.

6. Pattern evaluation to identify the truly interesting patterns representing knowledge based on some interestingness measures

7. Knowledge presentation where visualization and knowledge representation techniques are used to present the mined knowledge to the user.

1.3 Data mining

Data mining is the analysis of often large observational data sets to find unsuspected relationships and to summarize the data in novel ways that are both understandable and useful to data owner [15, 11]. It can refer to extracting or mining knowledge from large database. Statistics, database technology, machine learning, pattern recognition, artificial intelligence, and visualization, all play a role. In contrast to machine learning, the emphasis lies on the discovery of previously unknown patterns as opposed to generalizing known patterns to new data. They predict future trends and behaviours, allowing businesses to make proactive, knowledge-driven decisions.

The figure 1.2 describes that data mining and knowledge discovery in the data bases is a new interdisciplinary field, merging ideas from statistics, machine learning, databases and parallel computing.

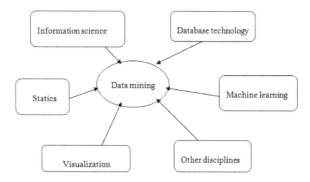

Figure 1.2 Data mining as a confluence of multiple disciplines

1.4 Data mining techniques

Data mining techniques have been developing and using in data mining projects recently including association, classification, clustering, prediction, sequential patterns and decision tree.

Association is one of the best known data mining technique. In association, a pattern is discovered based on a relationship between items in the same transaction. That's the reason why association technique is also known as relation technique. The association technique is used in market basket analysis to identify a set of products that customers frequently purchase together.

Classification is a classic data mining technique based on machine learning. Basically classification is used to classify each item in a set of data into one of predefined set of classes or groups. Classification method makes use of mathematical techniques such as decision trees, linear programming, neural network and statistics. In classification, we develop the software that can learn how to classify the data items into groups.

Clustering is a data mining technique that makes meaningful or useful cluster of objects which have similar characteristics using automatic technique. The clustering technique defines the classes and puts objects in each class, while in the classification techniques, objects are assigned into predefined classes.

3

The **prediction**, as it name implied, is one of a data mining techniques that discovers relationship between independent variables and relationship between dependent and independent variables. For instance, the prediction analysis technique can be used in sale to predict profit for the future if we consider sale is an independent variable, profit could be a dependent variable. Then based on the historical sale and profit data, we can draw a fitted regression curve that is used for profit prediction

1.5 Reality Mining

Reality mining is the collection and analysis of data where human social behaviour is analyzed through machine-sensed environment, with the goal of identifying predictable patterns of behaviour [12, 14]. It studies human interactions based on the usage of wireless devices such as mobile phones and GPS systems providing a more accurate picture of what people do, where they go, and with whom they communicate. It defines the collection of machine-sensed environmental data affecting to human social behaviour. This new paradigm of data mining makes possible the modelling of conversation context, proximity sensing, and temporal spatial location throughout large communities of individuals. Mobile phones (and similarly innocuous devices) are used for data collection, opening social network analysis to new methods of empirical stochastic modelling.

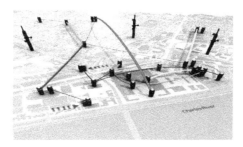

Figure 1.3 Visualization of the some of the Reality Mining data

The above Figure 1.3 describes about how people are connected in different location and records their human behaviour.

1.6   Objective of the work

- o   To study the drawback of existing decision tree algorithms.
- o   To construct decision tree technique using R software.
- o   To compare the decision tree with R using existing implementation.
- o   To apply and study the decision tree with reality mining.

1.7 Organization of the book

Initially, this chapter detailed about data mining, reality mining and decision tree concepts.

Chapter I discuss about the above mention terms in brief. These fundamental concepts will help us to understand clearly about their behaviour, and their properties etc. while completing this project.

Chapter II gives detailed and deep literature survey about classification, decision tree, ID3 algorithm. In this chapter how reality mining is beneficial for human being, it also describe that how we make our decision efficiently with decision tree.

Chapter III briefly describes about the R software, existing system, proposed system and system requirements. It also provides some sample codes with R.

Chapter IV elaborate about reality mining deeply as well as it also describes the different data sets used in reality mining.

Chapter V explain about how the algorithm works and what will get as an output using the ID3 algorithm in R.

CHAPTER II

LITERATURE SURVEY

2.1 Introduction

This chapter will discuss about the classification techniques and decision tree algorithm. This chapter provides detailed information about classification and decision tree. Classification is a data mining function that assigns items in a collection to target categories or classes. The goal of classification is to accurately predict the target class for each case in the data.

2.2 Classification

Classification is the process of finding a model that describe and distinguishes data classes, with the purpose of using model to predict the class of objects whose class label is unknown [3]. The model is based on analysis of set of training data. Data classification is a two step process:-

- Model construction:- describing a set of predetermined classes.
- Model usage:- for classifying future or unknown objects.

The data analysis task classification is where a model or classifier is constructed to predict categorical labels (the class label attributes) [11]. For example, Categorical labels include "safe" or "risky" for the loan application data. Data classification is a two-step process.

Step 1: A classifier is built describing a predetermined set of data classes or concepts. This is the learning step (or training phase), where a classification algorithm builds the classifier by analyzing or "learning from" a training set made up of database tuples and their associated class labels. Each tuple, is assumed to belong to a predefined class called the class label attribute. Because the class label of each training tuple is provided, this step is also known as supervised learning. The first step can also be viewed as the learning of a mapping or function, $y = f(X)$, that can predict the associated class label y of a given tuple X. Typically, this mapping is represented in the form of classification rules, decision trees, or mathematical formulae.

6

Step 2: Here, the model is used for classification. First, the predictive accuracy of the classifier is estimated. If we were to use the training set to measure the accuracy of the classifier, this estimate would likely be optimistic, because the classifier tends to overfit the data. Therefore, a test set is used, made up of test tuples and their associated class labels. The associated class label of each test tuple is compared with the learned classifier's class prediction for that tuple. If the accuracy of the classifier is considered acceptable, the classifier can be used to classify future data tuples for which the class label is not known. For example, the classification rules learned in Fig. from the analysis of data from previous loan applications can be used to approve or reject new or future loan applicants.

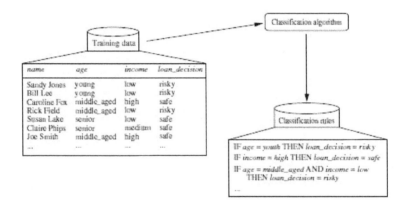

Figure 2.1 Data classification process step 1 learning

Figure 1.4 describes that training data are analysed by a classification algorithm. Here, the class label attribute is loan_decision , and the learned model or classifier is represented in the form of classification rules. Figure 1.5 describes that test data are used to estimate the accuracy of the classification rules. If accuracy is considered acceptable, the rules can be applied to the classification of new data tuples.

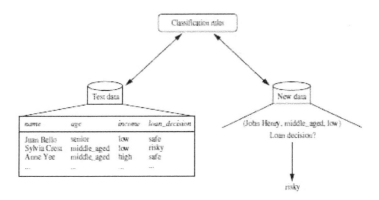

Figure 2.2 Data classification process step 2 classification

2.3 Types of classification

Several types of classification are their some of them are describing as follows:-

2.3.1 Bayesian classification

Bayesian classifiers are statistical classifiers which can predict class membership probabilities, such as the probability that a given tuple belong to a particular class.

2.3.2 Naive Bayesian classification

The naïve Bayes model is a simple and well known method for performing supervised learning of a classification problem. The naive Bayesian classifier makes the assumption of class conditional independence, i.e., given the class label of a tuple, the values of the attributes are assumed to be conditionally independent of one another.

This method is important for several reasons. It is very easy to construct, not needing any complicated iterative parameter estimation schemes [3, 15]. This means it may be readily applied to huge data sets. It is easy to interpret, so users unskilled in classifier technology can understand why it is making the classification it makes. And finally, it often does surprisingly well: it may not be the best possible classifier in any particular application, but it can usually be relied on to be robust and to do quite well.

The naive Bayes model is tremendously appealing because of its simplicity, elegance, and robustness. It is one of the oldest formal classification algorithms, and yet even in its

8

simplest form it is often surprisingly effective. It is widely used in areas such as text classification and spam filtering. A large number of modifications have been introduced, by the statistical, data mining, machine learning, and pattern recognition communities, in an attempt to make it more flexible, but one has to recognize that such modifications are necessarily complications, which detract from its basic simplicity.

2.3.3 Bayesian Belief Network

Bayesian belief network specify joint conditional probability distributions. They allow class conditional independencies to be defined between subsets of variables. They provide a graphical model of casual relationships, on which learning can be performed. Trained Bayesian belief networks can be used for classification.

A belief network is defined by two components

- A directed acyclic graph
- Conditional probability tables

RID	Credit_rating	Age	Buys_computer
1	Excellent	38	Yes
2	Excellent	26	Yes
3	Fair	35	No
4	Excellent	49	No

Table 2.1 Tuple data for the class buys_computer

2.3.4 Classification by Back Propagation

Backpropagation learns by iteratively processing a set of training samples, comparing the network's prediction for each sample with the actual known class label. For each training sample, the weights are modified so as to minimize the mean squared error between the networks prediction and the actual class [11]. The adjustments are made in the backward direction, that is, from the output layer through each hidden layer down to the first layer.

Method

(1)   Initialize all weights and biases in network;

(2)   While terminating condition is not satisfied

(3)   {

(4)   For each training sample X in samples {

(5)   // propagate the input forward:

9

(6)   for each hidden or output layer unit j

(7) $\{ I_j = \sum_i w_{ij} \ O_i + O_j$

(8) $O_j = 1/1 + e - I_j; \}$

(9)   // Backpropogate the errors:

(10)   For each unit j in the output layer

(11) $Err_j = O_j \ (1 - O_j)(T_j - O_j);$

(12)   For each unit j in the hidden layers, from the last to the first hidden layer

(13) $Err_j = O_j \ (1 - O_j) \sum Err_k \ W_{jk}$

(14)   For each weight W_{ij} in network {

(15) $\Delta W_{ij} = (1) \ Err_j \ O_i;$

(16) $W_{ij} = W_{ij} + \Delta W_{ij};$

(17)   For each bias Θ_j in network {

(18) $\Delta \Theta_j = (1) \ Err_j;$

(19) $\Theta_j = \Theta_j + \Delta \Theta_j$

(20)   }

(21)   }

2.3.5 k-nearest neighbour classification

k-nearest neighbour (kNN) classification, finds a group of k objects in the training set that are closest to the test object, and bases the assignment of a label on the predominance of a particular class in this neighbourhood. There are three key elements of this approach: a set of labelled objects, e.g., a set of stored records, a distance or similarity metric to compute distance between objects, and the value of k, the number of nearest neighbours. To classify an unlabeled object, the distance of this object to the labelled objects is computed, its k-nearest neighbours are identified, and the class labels of these nearest neighbours are then used to determine the class label of the object.

2.4 Decision tree

A decision tree is a tree in which each branch node represents a choice between a number of alternatives, and each leaf node represents a decision. They are commonly used for gaining information for the purpose of decision -making. It starts with a root node on which it is for users to take actions. From this node, users split each node recursively according to

10

decision tree learning algorithm [5, 7]. The final result is a decision tree in which each branch represents a possible scenario of decision and its outcome.

A decision tree is a decision support tool that uses a tree-like graph or model of decisions and their possible consequences, including chance event outcomes, resource costs, and utility. It is one way to display an algorithm. The most important feature of decision tree is their capability to break down a complex decision-making process into a collection of simpler decisions, thus providing a solution which is often easier to interpret. A decision strategy is a particular branch path in a decision tree and includes all the decisions and chance events along that branch path. This generally includes two or more possible decision strategies [8, 9]. Decision tree analysis is the process of evaluating alternative decision alternatives emanating from the root node. The analysis requires calculating and then comparing expected values.

2.5 Related works

This section will describe the several kinds of algorithm and their technique used for constructing a decision tree.

2.5.1 Decision Tree Induction

Decision tree induction is the learning of decision trees from class-labeled training tuples. A decision tree is a flowchart like tree structure, where each internal node denotes a test on an attribute, each branch represents an outcome of the test, and each leaf node holds a class label [11, 15]. The topmost node in a tree is the root node. Generally our input for generating decision tree from training tuples will be as follows:-

- A data partition, which is a set of training tuples and their associated class labels.
- The set of candidate attributes.
- Finally a procedure to determine the splitting criterion that best partitions the data tuples into individual classes.

The output contains:-

- A decision tree.

11

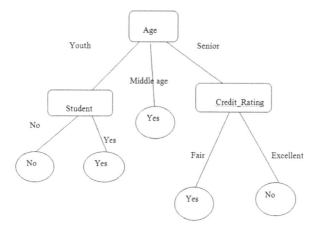

Figure 2.3 A Decision Tree

Method:-

1:    Create a node N;

2:    If tuples in D are all of the same class, C then,

3:    Return N as leaf node labeled with the class C;

4:    If attribute_list is empty then,

5:    Return N as a leaf node labeled with the majority class in D;

6:    Apply Attribute_selection_method (D,attribute list) to find the ―best‖ splitting_criterion;

7:    Label node N with splitting_criterion;

8:    If splitting_attribute is discrete-valued and multiway splits allowed then,

9:    Attribute_list=attribute list-splliting attribute;//remove splitting_attribute

10:   For each outcome j of splitting_criterion

11:   Let D_j be the set of data tuples in D satisfying outcome j;

12:   If D_j is empty then,

13:   Attach a leaf labeled with the majority class in D to node N;

14:   Else attach the node returned by Decision_Tree(D_j, attribute list) to node N;

15:   Endfor

16:   Return N;

The tree starts as a single node, N, representing the training tuple in D. If tuples in D are all of same class, then node N become a leaf node and labeled with that class, otherwise the algorithm call Attribute selection method to determine splitting criteria. The recursive portioning stop only when any one of following terminating condition is true:

1.   All the tuples in partition D belongs to same class.

2.   There are no remaining attributes on which tuple will further partitioned.

3.   There are no tuple for a given branch, i.e., a partition D_j is empty.

2.5.2 ID 3

ID3 is a simple decision tree learning algorithm developed by Ross Quinlan (1983). The basic idea of ID3 algorithm is to construct the decision tree by applying a top-down, greedy search through the given sets to test each attribute at every tree node.[4, 1] ID3 is mathematical algorithm for building the decision tree.

To find an optimal way to classify a learning set, what we need to do is to minimize the questions asked (i.e. minimizing the depth of the tree). Thus, we need some function which can measure which questions provide the most balanced splitting. The information gain metric is such a function.

SIZE	COLOR	SHAPE	CLASS
Small	Yellow	Round	A
Big	Yellow	Round	A
Big	Red	Round	A
Small	Red	Round	A
Small	Black	Round	B
Big	Black	Cube	B
Big	Yellow	Cube	B

Table 2.2 Tuple data for decision tree

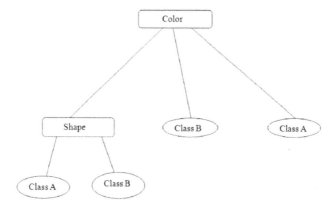

Figure 2.4 Decision tree generated by color attributes

2.5.2.1 Entropy

In order to define information gain precisely, we need to discuss entropy first. First, let's assume, without loss of generality, that the resulting decision tree classifies instances into two categories, we'll call them P (positive) and N (negative).

Given a set S, containing these positive and negative targets, the entropy of S related to this Boolean classification is:

Entropy(S) = - P (positive) log2P (positive) - P (negative) log2P (negative) P (positive): proportion of positive examples in S

P (negative): proportion of negative examples in S

2.5.2.2 Information Gain

To minimize the decision tree depth, when we traverse the tree path, we need to select the optimal attribute for splitting the tree node, which we can easily imply that the attribute with the most entropy reduction is the best choice.

We define information gain as the expected reduction of entropy related to specified attribute when splitting a decision tree node.

The information gain, Gain(S,A) of an attribute A,

Gain(S, A) = Entropy(S) - Sum for v from 1 to n of ($|Sv|/|S|$) * Entropy (Sv).

2.5.3 C4. 5

C4.5 generates classifiers expressed as decision trees, but it can also construct classifiers in more comprehensible rule set form. C4.5 uses two heuristic criteria to rank possible tests: information gain, which minimizes the total entropy of the subsets {Si } (but is heavily biased towards tests with numerous outcomes), and the default gain ratio that divides information gain by the information provided by the test outcomes [2].

Given a set S of cases, C4.5 first grows an initial tree using the divide-and-conquer algorithm as follows:

- If all the cases in S belong to the same class or S is small, the tree is a leaf labeled with the most frequent class in S.

- Otherwise, choose a test based on a single attribute with two or more outcomes. Make this test the root of the tree with one branch for each outcome of the test, partition S into corresponding subsets S1, S2, . . . according to the outcome for each case, and apply the same procedure recursively to each subset.

2.5.4 C5.0

C4.5 was superseded in 1997 by a commercial system See5/C5.0 (or C5.0 for short). The changes encompass new capabilities as well as much-improved efficiency, and include:

A variant of boosting, which constructs an ensemble of classifiers that are then voted to give a final classification. Boosting often leads to a dramatic improvement in predictive accuracy [1, 2].

- New data types (e.g., dates), ─not applicable‖ values, variable misclassification costs, and mechanisms to pre-filter attributes.

- Unordered rule sets—when a case is classified, all applicable rules are found and voted. This improves both the interpretability of rule sets and their predictive accuracy.

- Greatly improved scalability of both decision trees and (particularly) rule sets.

15

Scalability is enhanced by multi-threading; C5.0 can take advantage of computers with multiple CPUs and/or cores.

2.5.5 CART

The CART decision tree is a binary recursive partitioning procedure capable of processing continuous and nominal attributes both as targets and predictors. Data are handled in their raw form; no binning is required or recommended. Trees are grown to a maximal size without the use of a stopping rule and then pruned back (essentially split by split) to the root via cost-complexity pruning [3][7].

The next split to be pruned is the one contributing least to the overall performance of the tree on training data (and more than one split may be removed at a time). The procedure produces trees that are invariant under any order preserving transformation of the predictor attributes. This mechanism is intended to produce not one, but a sequence of nested pruned trees, all of which are candidate optimal trees.

The CART mechanism includes automatic (optional) class balancing, automatic missing value handling, and allows for cost-sensitive learning, dynamic feature construction, and probability tree estimation. It offers no internal performance measures for tree selection based on the training data as such measures are deemed suspect. Instead, tree performance is always measured on independent test data (or via cross validation) and tree selection proceeds only after test-data-based evaluation.

2.5.6 CHAID

CHAID is a type of decision tree technique, based upon adjusted significance testing (Bonferroni testing). The technique was developed in South Africa and was published in 1980 by Gordon V. Kass, who had completed a PhD thesis on this topic. CHAID can be used for prediction (in a similar fashion to regression analysis, this version of CHAID being originally known as XAID) as well as classification, and for detection of interaction between variables. CHAID stands for CHi-squared Automatic Interaction Detection, based upon a formal extension of the US AID (Automatic Interaction Detection) and THAID (THeta Automatic Interaction Detection) procedures of the 1960s and 70s, which in turn were extensions of earlier research, including that performed in the UK in the 1950s [8, 6].

16

In practice, CHAID is often used in the context of direct marketing to select groups of consumers and predict how their responses to some variables affect other variables, although other early applications were in the field of medical and psychiatric research.

Like other decision trees, CHAID's advantages are that its output is highly visual and easy to interpret. Because it uses multi way splits by default, it needs rather large sample sizes to work effectively, since with small sample sizes the respondent groups can quickly become too small for reliable analysis.

2.5.7 Tree Pruning

When a decision tree built many of the branches will reflect anomalies in the training data due to noise or outliers. Tree pruning method address this problem as over fitting the data. Such methods typically used statistical measures to remove the least reliable branches. Pruned tree tends to be less complex and, thus easier to comprehend [15]. They are usually faster and better at correctly classifying independent test than unpruned trees.

Two common approaches of tree pruning are:

- Prepruning
- Postpruning

In the **prepruning** approach, a tree is —pruned‖ by halting its construction early. Upon halting, the node becomes a leaf. The leaf may hold the most frequent class among the subset tuples or the probability distribution of those tuples. If partitioning the tuples at a node would result in a split that falls below a prespecificied threshold, then further partitioning of the given subset is halted.

In the postpruning approach, this removes subtrees from a —fully growth‖ tree. A subtree at a given node is pruned by removing its branches and replacing it with a leaf. The leaf is labeled with the most frequent class among the subtree being replaced.

17

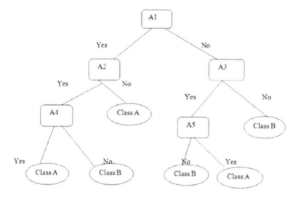

Figure 2.5 Unpruned Tree

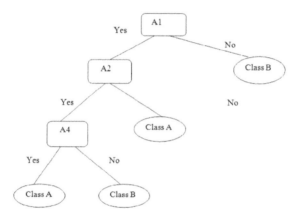

Figure 2.6 Pruned decision tree

2.6 Discussion about previous algorithm

ID3 is a simple decision tree learning algorithm developed by Ross Quinlan (1983). The Concept Learning System (CLS) algorithm is the basis for the ID3 algorithm. By adding a feature selection heuristic ID3 improves on CLS. The attributes of the training instances are searched through by ID3 and the attribute that best separates the given examples is extracted by it. ID3 stops if the attribute perfectly classifies the training sets; otherwise it recursively operates on the n, where n is the number of possible values of an attribute of the partitioned subsets to get their "best" attribute. A greedy search strategy is used by the algorithm; the

18

best attribute is picked by it and never reconsiders earlier choices by looking back.

CART algorithm stands for Classification and Regression Trees algorithm. It is a data exploration and prediction algorithm. Classification and Regression Trees is a classification method which in order to construct decision trees uses historical data. Then in order to classify new data decision trees so obtained are used. Number of classes must be known a priori in order to use CART. CART uses so called learning sample which is a set of historical data with pre-assigned classes for all observations for building decision trees.

CART and ID3, C4.5, C5.0 differs in the way splits are preformed. CART is a binary tree where the others are not. That means CART will choose several discrete values to split on. For example, if a feature is {red, green, blue} it could split on {red, green} on the left and {blue} on the right or any combination of the 3. CART also handles discrete as well as continuous values too.

2.7 Research issues
In the following section certain research issues related to this project has been discussed.

2.7.1 Challenges and Issues in Decision Tree
A decision tree can be used to clarify and find an answer to a complex problem. The structure allows users to take a problem with multiple possible solutions and display it in a simple, easy-to-understand format that shows the relationship between different events or decisions.

Following are the research issues in decision tree.

- Overfitting the data
- Guarding against bad attribute choices
- Handling continuous valued attributes
- Handling missing attribute values
- Handling attributes with differing costs

2.7.2 Disadvantages and Advantages of ID3 algorithm

Advantages of ID3 are:-

- Understandable and predictable rules are created from training data set.

19

- Build short tree.
- Finding leaf nodes enable test data to be pruned, reducing number of test.

Drawbacks of ID3 are:-

- Data may be over-fitted or over-classified, if a small sample is tested.
- Only one attribute at a time is tested for making decision.

To overcome these demerits, we are enhancing the ID3 algorithm by taking partial dataset to construct decision tree and rest dataset will be used to examine a decision tree.

2.7.3 Advantages and Disadvantage of reality mining

Consider two examples of how reality mining may benefit individual health care.

By taking advantage of special sensors in mobile phones, such as the microphone or the accelerometers built into newer devices like Apple's iPhone, important diagnostic data can be captured. Commercial trials by start-up cogito health are demonstrating that we can accurately screen for depression from the way a person talks -- depressed people tend to speak more slowly, a change that speech analysis software on a phone might recognize more readily than friends or family do.

Similarly, experiments in some laboratory have shown that monitoring a phone's motion sensors can also reveal small changes in gait, which could be an early indicator of ailments such as Parkinson's disease.

Disadvantage of reality mining can be says as —reality mining collect individual data, such data can also become a potential threat to individual privacy.

2.8 Summary

This chapter deals with detailed information about various decision tree algorithm and techniques and it also explain about the research issues related to decision tree and reality mining. It describe briefly about the classification and its types and their techniques. Decision tree is one of the techniques of classification that is also described briefly.

CHAPTER III
ITERATIVE DICHOTOMISER 3

3.1 Introduction

This chapter briefly explain the existing and proposed system of the project. Also it will give a brief explanation of the technology that is used in the project.

3.2 Problem Description

The input data for a classification task is a collection of records. Each record, also known as an instance or example, is characterized by a tuple (X, y), where X is a attribute set and y is a special attribute, designated as the class label. A classification model can serve as an explanatory tool to distinguish between objects of different classes. The training set is used to build a classification model, which is subsequently applied to the test set, which consist of records with unknown class labels.

To illustrate how classification with a decision tree works, consider a simple version of the vertebrate classification problem described in the previous section. Instead of classifying the vertebrate into five distinct groups of species, we assign them to two categories: mammals and non-mammals.

Suppose a new species is discovered by scientists. How can we tell whether it is a mammal or non- mammals? One approach is to pose a series of questions about the characteristics of the species. The first question we may ask is whether the species is cold or warm blooded. If it is cold-blooded, then it is definitely not a mammal. Otherwise, it is either a bird or a mammal. In the latter case, we need to ask a follow-up questions : Do the female of the species give birth to their young? Those that do give birth are definitely mammals with exception of egg-laying mammals such as the platypus and spiny anteater.

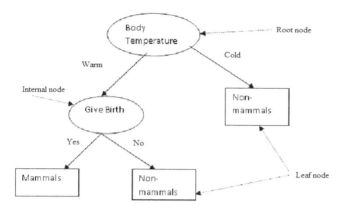

Figure 3.1 A decision tree for mammal classification problem

3.3 Existing System

Classification techniques are most suited for predicting or describing data sets with binary and nominal categories. They are less effective for ordinal categories because they will not consider the implicit order among the categories.

It is a systematic approach to building classification models from an input data set such as decision tree classifier, rule-based classifier, neural networks, and support vector machine. Each technique employs a learning algorithm to identify a model that best fits the relationship between the attribute set and class label of the input data [6]. The model generated by a learning algorithm should both fit the input data well and correctly predict the class labels of records it has never seen before.

Decision tree is a simple but widely used classification technique. In decision tree each leaf node is assigned a class label. The non- terminal node, which include root and other internal node contain attribute test conditions to separate records that have different characteristics.

There are exponentially many decision trees that can be constructed from a given set of attributes. While some of the trees are more accurate than others, finding the optimal tree is computationally infeasible because of the exponential size of the search space. Nevertheless efficient algorithms have been developed to induce a reasonably accurate, decision tree in a reasonable amount of time [9]. These algorithms usually employ a greedy strategy that grows a decision tree by making a series of locally optimum decision about which attribute t be used for portioning the data such as ID3, C4.5, and CART.

3.4 Proposed System

3.4.1 R Software

R is a system for statistical computation and graphics. It provides, among other things, a programming language, high level graphics, interfaces to other languages and debugging facilities. The R language is a dialect of S which was designed in the 1980s and has been in widespread use in the statistical community since. Its principal designer, John M. Chambers, was awarded the 1998 ACM Software Systems Award for S [16, 17].

The language syntax has a superficial similarity with C, but the semantics are of the FPL (functional programming language) variety with stronger affinities with Lisp and APL. In particular, it allows "computing on the language", which in turn makes it possible to write functions that take expressions as input, something that is often useful for statistical modelling and graphics. There are about 25 packages supplied with R (called "standard" and "recommended" packages) and many more are available through the CRAN family of Internet sites (via http://CRAN.R-project.org) and elsewhere.

3.4.2 ID3 using R

R is an integrated suite of software facilities for data manipulation, calculation and graphical display [16]. Among other things it has an effective data handling and storage facility, a suite of operators for calculations on arrays, in particular matrices, a large, coherent, integrated collection of intermediate tools for data analysis, graphical facilities for data analysis and display either directly at the computer or on hardcopy, and a well developed, simple and effective programming language (called 'S') which includes conditionals, loops, user defined recursive functions and input and output facilities.

ID3 is a simple decision learning algorithm developed by J. Ross Quinlan. ID3 constructs decision tree by employing a top-down, greedy search through the given sets of training data to test each attribute at every node. It uses statistical property call information gain to select which attribute to test at each node in the tree. Information gain measures how well a given attribute separates the training examples according to their target classification.

Here ID3 algorithm is applied with R Software. The pseudo code for ID3 is as follows:

ID3 (Examples, Target_Attribute, Attributes)

Create a root node for the tree

If all examples are positive, Return the single-node tree Root, with label= +.

If all examples are negative, Return the single-node tree Root, with label = -.

If number of predicting attributes is empty, then Return the single node tree Root, with label = most common value of the target attribute in the examples.

Otherwise Begin

$A \leftarrow$ The Attribute that best classifies examples.

Decision Tree attribute for Root = A.

For each possible value, v_i, of A,

Add a new tree branch below Root, corresponding to the test A = v_i.

Let Examples (v_i) be the subset of examples that have the value v_i for A

If Examples (v_i) is empty

Then below this new branch add a leaf node with label = most common target value in the examples

Else below this new branch add the subtree ID3 (Examples (v_i), Target_Attribute, Attributes – {A})

End

Return Root

There are a couple of R packages on decision trees, such as party, rpart, random forest. Here the decision tree starts to build with party package and Iris data set. In the package, function ctree() builds a decision tree, and predict() makes prediction for unlabeled data.

The flowchart of function conditional tree (ctree()) explain the process of constructing decision tree with R software. In given flow chart firstly the fitting procedure will take place, and then it will grow the tree. Class S3 is created which contain all the method of growing a tree and fitting it. If the data is unlabeled then it put the name on list to label it. Then learning sample will be crated and memory is set up to store that sample. Finally learning sample data is fitted and it will return a conditional tree.

24

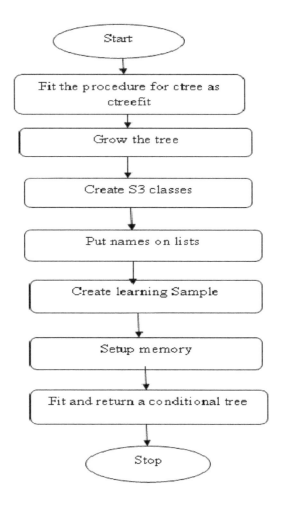

Figure 3.2 Flowchart for function ctree()

3.5 Hardware and Software Requirements

Hardware Requirements

System: Pentium IV 2.4 GHz

Hardware: 120 GB

RAM: 512 MB

25

Software Requirement

Operating System: Windows XP

Tool: R Software 32/62 bit 2.5.2.1 Version

3.6 Summary

This chapter describes the problem of project as well as it's also elaborate about the existing and proposed system. It explain about the software used in project as well as it also specify the hardware and software requirement of system.

CHAPTER IV

REALITY MINING

4.1 Introduction

This chapter will elaborate the concept of reality mining and the data sets used for reality mining, which has been collected by the usage of mobile to study the behaviour of human and others.

4.2 Reality Mining

Reality mining studies human interactions based on the usage of wireless devices such as mobile phones and GPS systems providing a more accurate picture of what people do, where they go, and with whom they communicate with rather than from more subjective sources such as a person's own account [10, 11]. Reality mining is one aspect of digital footprint analysis. Around the world, many of us live our lives in digital networks. We wake up in the morning, check our email, make a quick phone call, commute to work, and buy lunch. Many of these transactions leave digital bread-crumbs—tiny records of our daily experiences. Reality mining, which pulls together these crumbs using statistical analysis and machine learning methods, offers increasingly extensive information about our lives, both individually and collectively.

Reality mining of behaviour data is just beginning. For instance, the correlation of behaviour data with medication data from millions of people could make drug therapies more effective and help medical professionals detect drug interactions more quickly. If behaviour data were correlated with medical conditions, the data could illuminate the etiologic and preconditions of disease far more powerfully than is possible today and, further, serve as an early warning system for epidemic diseases.

4.3 Data Sets

The data sets are as follows :

- Iris Data Set

Iris data set consists of information on 150 Iris flower, 50 each from one of three Iris species: Setosa, Versicolour, and Virginica. Each flower is characterized by five attributes:

27

- Sepal length in centimetres
- Sepal width in centimetres
- Petal length in centimetres
- Petal width in centimetres
- Class (Setosa, Versicolour, Verginica)

> str(iris)

'data.frame': 150 obs. of 5 variables:

$ Sepal.Length: num 5.1 4.9 4.7 4.6 5 5.4 4.6 5 4.4 4.9 ...

$ Sepal.Width : num 3.5 3 3.2 3.1 3.6 3.9 3.4 3.4 2.9 3.1 ...

$ Petal.Length: num 1.4 1.4 1.3 1.5 1.4 1.7 1.4 1.5 1.4 1.5 ...

$ Petal.Width : num 0.2 0.2 0.2 0.2 0.2 0.4 0.3 0.2 0.2 0.1 ...

$ Species : Factor w/ 3 levels "setosa","versicolor",..: 1 1 1 1 1 1 1 1 1 1 ...

- Bodyfat Data Set

Bodyfat is a dataset contain 71 rows, in which each row contains information of one person. It contains the following 10 numeric columns.

• age: age in years.

• DEXfat: body fat measured by DXA, response variable.

• waistcirc: waist circumference.

• hipcirc: hip circumference.

• elbowbreadth: breadth of the elbow.

• kneebreadth: breadth of the knee.

• anthro3a: sum of logarithm of three anthropometric measurements.

• anthro3b: sum of logarithm of three anthropometric measurements.

• anthro3c: sum of logarithm of three anthropometric measurements.

• anthro4: sum of logarithm of three anthropometric measurements

> str(bodyfat)

'data.frame': 71 obs. of 10 variables:

$ age : num 57 65 59 58 60 61 56 60 58 62 ...

$ DEXfat : num 41.7 43.3 35.4 22.8 36.4 ...

$ waistcirc : num 100 99.5 96 72 89.5 83.5 81 89 80 79 ...

$ hipcirc : num 112 116.5 108.5 96.5 100.5 ...

$ elbowbreadth: num 7.1 6.5 6.2 6.1 7.1 6.5 6.9 6.2 6.4 7 ...

$ kneebreadth : num 9.4 8.9 8.9 9.2 10 8.8 8.9 8.5 8.8 8.8 ...

$ anthro3a : num 4.42 4.63 4.12 4.03 4.24 3.55 4.14 4.04 3.91 3.66 ...

$ anthro3b : num 4.95 5.01 4.74 4.48 4.68 4.06 4.52 4.7 4.32 4.21 ...

$ anthro3c : num 4.5 4.48 4.6 3.91 4.15 3.64 4.31 4.47 3.47 3.6 ...

$ anthro4 : num 6.13 6.37 5.82 5.66 5.91 5.14 5.69 5.7 5.49 5.25

- Titanic Data Set

The Titanic dataset in the datasets package is a 4-dimensional table with summarized information on the fate of passengers on the Titanic according to social class, sex, age and survival.

> str(Titanic)

table [1:4, 1:2, 1:2, 1:2] 0 0 35 0 0 0 17 0 118 154 ...

- attr(*, "dimnames")=List of 4

..$ Class : chr [1:4] "1st" "2nd" "3rd" "Crew"

..$ Sex : chr [1:2] "Male" "Female"

..$ Age : chr [1:2] "Child" "Adult"

..$ Survived: chr [1:2] "No" "Yes"

4.4 Summary

This chapter discuss briefly about reality mining and various types of data sets used for reality mining to build a decision tree, and it's also clarify the concept of reality mining data sets which has been collected by sensor in a real time environment.

CHAPTER V

RESULT AND DISCUSSION

5.1 Introduction

This chapter will discuss briefly about how an effective decision tree can be constructed using ID3 algorithm. To illustrate with an output of decision tree, let's take Iris data set to build the tree.

5.2 Algorithm for Decision Tree

A skeleton decision tree induction algorithm called TreeGrowth is shown in Algorithm. The input to this algorithm consists of the training records E and the attribute set F. The algorithm works by recursively selecting the best attribute to split the data and expanding the leaf nodes of the tree until the stopping criterion is met.

TreeGrowth(E,F)

if stopping_cond(E,F)=true then

leaf=createNode().

leaf.label=Classify(E).

return leaf

else

root=createNode().

root.test_cond=find_best_split(E,F).

let V={v|v is a possible outcome of root.test_cond}

for each v ∈V do

Ev ={e| root.test_cond (e)= v and e ∈ E}

child = TreeGrowth (Ev,F).

add child as descendent of root and label the edge (root→child)as v

end for

end if

return root

The details of this algorithm are explained below:

1. The createNode() function extends the decision tree by creating a new node. A node in the decision tree has either a test condition, denoted as node.test_cond, or a class label, denoted as node.label.

.2. The find_best_split() function determines which attribute should be selected as the test condition for splitting the training records. As previously noted, the choice of test condition depends on which impurity measure is used to determine the goodness of a split. Some widely used measures include entropy, the Gini index.

3. The Classify() function determines the class label to be assigned to a leaf node.

4. The stopping_cond() function is used to terminate the tree-growing process by testing whether all the records have either the same class label or the same attribute values. Another way to terminate the recursive function is to test whether the numbers of records have fallen below some minimum threshold.

After building the decision tree, a tree-pruning step can be performed to reduce the size of the decision tree. Decision trees that arc too large are susceptible to a phenomenon known as overfitting. Pruning helps by trimming the branches of the initial tree in a way that improves the generalization capability of the decision tree.

5.3 Building Decision tree with R

R is open source software, which contain certain package. With party package decision tree is constructed with its two function ctree() to build tree and predict() make prediction for unlabed data.

The Iris data set is split into two subsets: training (70%) and testing (30%).With the following R code using ID3 algorithm the result will be as follows

```
> set.seed(1234)

> ind <- sample(2, nrow(iris), replace=TRUE, prob=c(0.7, 0.3))

> trainData <- iris[ind==1,]

> testData <- iris[ind==2,]
```

Load package party, build a decision tree, and check the prediction.

```
> library(party)
```

```
> myFormula <- Species ~ Sepal.Length + Sepal.Width + Petal.Length + Petal.Width
> iris_ctree <- ctree(myFormula, data=trainData)
> # check the prediction
> table(predict(iris_ctree), trainData$Species)
```

To plot an decision tree:

```
>plot(iris_ctree)
```

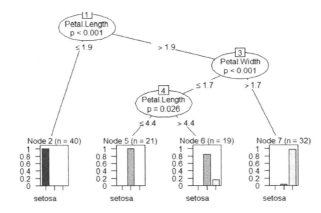

Figure 5.1 Decision tree for iris data set

```
>plot(iris_ctree, type="simple")
```

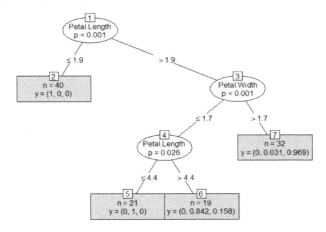

Figure 5.2 Simple Decision tree for iris

33

5.4 Sample code

 # For building tree ctree()

```
-`ctreefit <- function(object, controls, weights = NULL, fitmem = NULL, ...) {
if (!extends(class(object), "LearningSample"))
stop (sQuote("object"), " is not of class ", sQuote("LearningSample"))
if (!extends(class(controls), "TreeControl"))
stop(sQuote("controls"), " is not of class ", sQuote("TreeControl"))
if (is.null(fitmem))
fitmem <- ctree_memory(object, TRUE)
if (!extends(class(fitmem), "TreeFitMemory"))
stop(sQuote("fitmem"), " is not of class ", sQuote("TreeFitMemory"))
if (is.null(weights))
weights <- object@weights
storage.mode(weights) <- "double"
if (length(weights) != object@nobs || storage.mode(weights) != "double")
stop(sQuote("weights"), " are not a double vector of ",
object@nobs, " elements")
if (max(abs(floor(weights) -  weights)) > sqrt(.Machine$double.eps))
stop(sQuote("weights"), " contains real valued elements; currently
only integer values are allowed")
where <- rep(0, object@nobs)
storage.mode(where) <- "integer"
tree <- .Call("R_TreeGrow", object, weights, fitmem, controls, where,
PACKAGE = "party")
tree <- prettytree(tree, names(object@inputs@variables),
object@inputs@levels)
RET <- new("BinaryTree")
RET@tree <- tree
RET@where <- where
RET@weights <- weights
RET@responses <- object@responses
if (inherits(object, "LearningSampleFormula"))
```

```r
RET@data <- object@menv
RET@update <- function(weights = NULL) {
ctreefit(object = object, controls = controls,
weights = weights, fitmem = fitmem, ...)
}
RET@get_where <- function(newdata = NULL, mincriterion = 0, ...) {
if (is.null(newdata) && mincriterion == 0) {
if (all(where > 0)) return(where)
}
newinp <- newinputs(object, newdata)
.Call("R_get_nodeID", tree, newinp, mincriterion, PACKAGE = "party")
}
RET@cond_distr_response <- function(newdata = NULL, mincriterion = 0, ...) {
wh <- RET@get_where(newdata = newdata, mincriterion = mincriterion)
response <- object@responses
if (any(response@is_censored)) {
swh <- sort(unique(wh))
# w <- .Call("R_getweights", tree, swh,
# PACKAGE = "party")
RET <- vector(mode = "list", length = length(wh))
resp <- response@variables[[1]]
for (i in 1:length(swh)) {
w <- weights * (where == swh[i])
RET[wh == swh[i]] <- list(mysurvfit(resp, weights = w))
}
return(RET)
}
RET <- .Call("R_getpredictions", tree, wh, PACKAGE = "party")
return(RET)
}
RET@predict_response <- function(newdata = NULL, mincriterion = 0,
type = c("response", "node", "prob"), ...) {
type <- match.arg(type)
```

```r
if (type == "node")
return(RET@get_where(newdata = newdata,
mincriterion = mincriterion, ...))
cdresp <- RET@cond_distr_response(newdata = newdata,
mincriterion = mincriterion, ...)
if (type == "prob")
return(cdresp)
if (object@responses@ninputs > 1)
return(cdresp)
response <- object@responses
if (all(response@is_nominal || response@is_ordinal)) {
lev <- levels(response@variables[[1]])
RET <- factor(lev[unlist(lapply(cdresp, which.max))],
levels = levels(response@variables[[1]]))
return(RET) }
if (any(response@is_censored)) {
RET <- sapply(cdresp, mst)
return(RET)
}
RET <- unlist(cdresp)
RET <- matrix(unlist(RET),
nrow = length(RET), byrow = TRUE)
if (response@ninputs == 1)
colnames(RET) <- names(response@variables)
return(RET)
}
RET@prediction_weights <- function(newdata = NULL,
mincriterion = 0, ...) {
wh <- RET@get_where(newdata = newdata, mincriterion = mincriterion)
swh <- sort(unique(wh))
# w <- .Call("R_getweights", tree, swh,
# PACKAGE = "party")
RET <- vector(mode = "list", length = length(wh))
```

```
for (i in 1:length(swh))
RET[wh == swh[i]] <- list(weights * (where == swh[i]))
return(RET)
}
return(RET)
}
ctreedpp <- function(formula, data = list(), subset = NULL,
na.action = NULL, xtrafo = ptrafo, ytrafo = ptrafo,
scores = NULL, ...) {
dat <- ModelEnvFormula(formula = formula, data = data,
subset = subset, designMatrix = FALSE,
responseMatrix = FALSE, ...)
inp <- initVariableFrame(dat@get("input"), trafo = xtrafo,
scores = scores)
response <- dat@get("response")
if (any(is.na(response)))
stop("missing values in response variable not allowed")
resp <- initVariableFrame(response, trafo = ytrafo, response = TRUE)
RET <- new("LearningSampleFormula", inputs = inp, responses = resp,
weights = rep(1, inp@nobs), nobs = inp@nobs,
ninputs = inp@ninputs, menv = dat)
RET
}
conditionalTree <- new("StatModel",
capabilities = new("StatModelCapabilities"),
name = "unbiased conditional recursive partitioning",
dpp = ctreedpp,
fit = ctreefit,
predict = function(object, ...)
object@predict_response(...) )
setMethod("fit", signature = signature(model = "StatModel",
data = "LearningSample"),
definition = function(model, data, ...)
```

```
model@fit(data, ...)
)
ctree_control <- function(teststat = c("quad", "max"
testtype = c("Bonferroni", "MonteCarlo", "Univariate", "Teststatistic"),
mincriterion = 0.95, minsplit = 20, minbucket = 7, stump = FALSE,
nresample = 9999, maxsurrogate = 0, mtry = 0,
savesplitstats = TRUE, maxdepth = 0) {
teststat <- match.arg(teststat)
testtype <- match.arg(testtype)
RET <- new("TreeControl")
if (teststat %in% levels(RET@varctrl@teststat)) {
RET@varctrl@teststat <- factor(teststat,
levels = levels(RET@varctrl@teststat))
} else {
 stop(sQuote("teststat"), teststat, " not defined")
}
if (testtype %in% levels(RET@gtctrl@testtype))
RET@gtctrl@testtype <- factor(testtype,
levels = levels(RET@gtctrl@testtype))
else
stop(testtype, " not defined")
if (RET@gtctrl@testtype == "Teststatistic")
RET@varctrl@pvalue <- FALSE
RET@gtctrl@nresample <- as.integer(nresample)
RET@gtctrl@mincriterion <- mincriterion
if (all(mtry > 0)) {
RET@gtctrl@randomsplits <- TRUE
RET@gtctrl@mtry <- as.integer(mtry)
}
RET@tgctrl@savesplitstats <- savesplitstats
RET@splitctrl@minsplit <- minsplit
RET@splitctrl@maxsurrogate <- as.integer(maxsurrogate)
RET@splitctrl@minbucket <- as.double(minbucket)
```

```
RET@splitctrl@minbucket <- as.double(minbucket)
```

```
RET@tgctrl@stump <- stump
RET@tgctrl@maxdepth <- as.integer(maxdepth)
RET@tgctrl@savesplitstats <- savesplitstats
if (!validObject(RET))
stop("RET is not a valid object of class", class(RET))
RET }
ctree <- function(formula, data = list(), subset = NULL, weights = NULL,
controls = ctree_control(), xtrafo = ptrafo,
ytrafo = ptrafo, scores = NULL) {
ls <- dpp(conditionalTree, formula, data, subset, xtrafo = xtrafo,
ytrafo = ytrafo, scores = scores)
fitmem <- ctree_memory(ls, TRUE)
fit(conditionalTree, ls, controls = controls, weights = weights,
fitmem = fitmem)}


# For predict unlabel data predict()
predict.BinaryTree <- function(object, ...) {
conditionalTree@predict(object, ...)
}
predict.RandomForest <- function(object, OOB = FALSE, ...) {
RandomForest@predict(object, OOB = OOB, ...)
}
setGeneric("treeresponse", function(object, ...)
standardGeneric("treeresponse"))
setMethod("treeresponse", signature = signature(object = "BinaryTree"),
definition = function(object, newdata = NULL, ...)
object@cond_distr_response(newdata = newdata, ...)
)
setMethod("treeresponse", signature = signature(object = "RandomForest"),
definition = function(object, newdata = NULL, ...)
object@cond_distr_response(newdata = newdata, ...)
)
weights.BinaryTree <- function(object, newdata = NULL, ...)
```

```
object@prediction_weights(newdata = newdata, ...)
weights.RandomForest <- function(object, newdata = NULL, OOB = FALSE, ...)
object@prediction_weights(newdata = newdata, OOB = OOB, ...)
setGeneric("where", function(object, ...) standardGeneric("where"))
setMethod("where", signature = signature(object = "BinaryTree"),
definition = function(object, newdata = NULL, ...) {
if(is.null(newdata)) object@where
else object@get_where(newdata = newdata, ...)
}
)
setMethod("where", signature = signature(object = "RandomForest"),
definition = function(object, newdata = NULL, ...) {
 if(is.null(newdata)) object@where
else object@get_where(newdata = newdata, ...)
})
setGeneric("nodes", function(object, where, ...) standardGeneric("nodes"))
setMethod("nodes", signature = signature(object = "BinaryTree",
where = "integer"),
definition = function(object, where, ...)
 lapply(where, function(i) .Call("R_get_nodebynum", object@tree, i))
)
setMethod("nodes", signature = signature(object = "BinaryTree",
where = "numeric"),
definition = function(object, where, ...)
nodes(object, as.integer(where))
)
```

For printing an tree

```
prettysplit <- function(x, inames = NULL, ilevels = NULL) {
if (length(x) == 4)
names(x) <- c("variableID", "ordered", "splitpoint", "splitstatistics")
if (length(x) == 5)
```

40

```
names(x) <- c("variableID", "ordered", "splitpoint", "splitstatistics",
"toleft")
if (length(x) == 6)
names(x) <- c("variableID", "ordered", "splitpoint", "splitstatistics",
"toleft", "table")
if (x$ordered) {
class(x) <- "orderedSplit"
} else {
class(x) <- "nominalSplit"
}
if (!is.null(ilevels)) {
if (!is.null(ilevels[x[["variableID"]]]))
attr(x$splitpoint, "levels") <- ilevels[[x[["variableID"]]]]
}
if (!is.null(inames)) x$variableName <- inames[x[["variableID"]]]
return(x) }
prettytree <- function(x, inames = NULL, ilevels = NULL) {
names(x) <- c("nodeID", "weights", "criterion", "terminal",
"psplit", "ssplits", "prediction", "left", "right")
if (is.null(inames) && extends(class(x), "BinaryTree"))
inames <- names(x@data@get("input"))
names(x$criterion) <- c("statistic", "criterion", "maxcriterion")
names(x$criterion$criterion) <- inames
names(x$criterion$statistic) <- inames
if (x$terminal) {
class(x) <- "TerminalNode"
return(x)
}
x$psplit <- prettysplit(x$psplit, inames = inames, ilevels = ilevels)
if (length(x$ssplit) > 0)
x$ssplit <- lapply(x$ssplit, prettysplit, inames = inames,
ilevels = ilevels)
class(x) <- "SplittingNode"
```

```
x$left <- prettytree(x$left, inames = inames, ilevels = ilevels)
x$right <- prettytree(x$right, inames = inames, ilevels = ilevels)
return(x)
}
print.TerminalNode <- function(x, n = 1, ...) {
cat(paste(paste(rep(" ", n - 1), collapse = ""), x$nodeID, ")* ",
sep = "", collapse = ""),
"weights =", sum(x$weights), "\n")
}
print.SplittingNode <- function(x, n = 1, ...) {
cat(paste(paste(rep(" ", n - 1), collapse = ""), x$nodeID, ") ", sep=""))
print(x$psplit, left = TRUE)
cat(paste("; criterion = ", round(x$criterion$maxcriterion, 3),
 ", statistic = ", round(max(x$criterion$statistic), 3), "\n",
collapse = "", sep = ""))
print(x$left, n + 2)
cat(paste(paste(rep(" ", n - 1), collapse = ""), x$nodeID, ") ", sep=""))
print(x$psplit, left = FALSE)
cat("\n")
print(x$right, n + 2)
}
print.orderedSplit <- function(x, left = TRUE, ...) {
if (!is.null(attr(x$splitpoint, "levels"))) {
sp <- attr(x$splitpoint, "levels")[x$splitpoint]
} else {
sp <- x$splitpoint
}
if (!is.null(x$toleft)) left <- as.logical(x$toleft) == left
if (left) {
cat(x$variableName, "<=", sp)
} else {
cat(x$variableName, ">", sp)
}
```

```r
}
print.nominalSplit <- function(x, left = TRUE, ...) {
levels <- attr(x$splitpoint, "levels")
tab <- x$table
if (left) {
lev <- levels[as.logical(x$splitpoint) & (tab > 0)]
} else {
lev <- levels[!as.logical(x$splitpoint) & (tab > 0)]
}
txt <- paste("{", paste(lev, collapse = ", "), "}", collapse = "", sep = "")
cat(x$variableName, "==", txt)
}
print.BinaryTreePartition <- function(x, ...)
print(x@tree)
print.BinaryTree <- function(x, ...) {
cat("\n")
cat("\t Conditional inference tree with", length(unique(where(x))),
"terminal nodes\n\n")
y <- x@responses
if (y@ninputs > 1) {
cat("Responses:", paste(names(y@variables),
collapse = ", "), "\n")
} else {
cat("Response: ", names(y@variables), "\n")
}
inames <- names(x@data@get("input"))
if (length(inames) > 1) {
cat("Inputs: ", paste(inames, collapse = ", "), "\n")
} else {
cat("Input: ", inames, "\n")
}
cat("Number of observations: ", x@responses@nobs, "\n\n")
print(x@tree) }
```

```
print.RandomForest <- function(x, ...) {
cat("\n"
cat("\t Random Forest using Conditional Inference Trees\n")
cat("\n")
cat("Number of trees: ", length(x@ensemble), "\n")
cat("\n")
y <- x@responses
if (y@ninputs > 1) {
cat("Responses:", paste(names(y@variables),
collapse = ", "), "\n")
} else {
cat("Response: ", names(y@variables), "\n")
}
inames <- names(x@data@get("input"))
if (length(inames) > 1) {
cat("Inputs: ", paste(inames, collapse = ", "), "\n")
} else {
cat("Input: ", inames, "\n")
}
cat("Number of observations: ", x@responses@nobs, "\n\n")
invisible(x)
}
setMethod("show", "BinaryTree", function(object) print(object))
setMethod("show", "RandomForest", function(object) print(object))
```

5.5 Summary

This chapter briefly discuss about how algorithm will work, what will be the input and what will be output of the project. It also explains about how R software will construct decision tree and produce an output.

CHAPTER VI

CONCLUSION AND FUTURE ENHANCEMENT

6.1 Conclusion

This project present a novel, efficient and effective decision tree algorithm based on ID3 algorithm and gives an analysis on the significance of decision tree. The classical decision tree algorithm is modified (based on ID3) to build decision tree. The aim of this project is to demonstrate that the technology for building decision tree from example is moderately robust. ID3 is easy to use. Its primary use is replacing the expert who would normally build a classification tree by hand. As industry has shown, ID3 has been effective.

This project also concludes that ID3 works fairly well on classification problems. But there are some drawbacks in ID3 algorithm, which has been studied. The decision tree technique has been used and constructed using R Software. With existing implementation comparison is made for decision tree with R. Decision tree is studied with reality mining, the data sets are applied and studied to build decision tree for real data.

6.2 Future Enhancement

This work studied the performance of ID3 with R. The following future direction may be taken further,

- Implement with new or old measure
- Test with the real time dataset
- May compare with the other Decision Tree algorithm

APPENDIX I

Code in R for printing decision tree

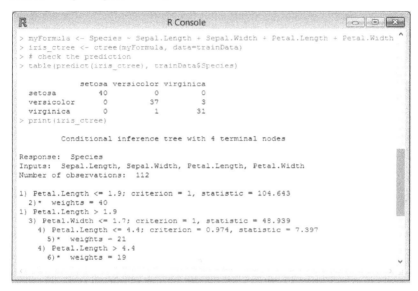

Output decision tree for iris data set

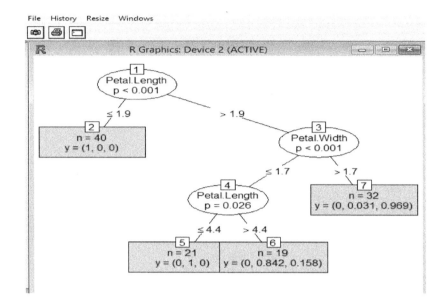

REFERENCES

[1] J. R. Quinlan, —Induction of decision trees,‖ Mach. Learn., vol. 1, no. 1, pp. 81–106, 1986.

[2] J.R. Quinlan, C4.5: Programs for Machine Learning. Morgan Kaufmann, 1993.

[3] L. Breiman et al. Classification and Regression Trees. Chapman and Hall,1993.

[4] A. Pentland, —Reality mining of mobile communications Global Information Technology Report: Toward a new deal on data,‖ The 2008-2009, 2008.

[5] Xi-Zhao Wang, Senior Member, IEEE, Ling-Cai Dong, Student Member, IEEE, and Jian-Hui Yan "Maximum Ambiguity-Based Sample Selection in Fuzzy Decision Tree Induction" IEEE transactions on knowledge and data engineering, vol. 24, no. 8, august 2012.

[6] J. Dem_sar, —Statistical Comparisons of Classifiers over Multiple Data Sets,‖ J Machine Learning Research, vol. 7, pp.1-30, 2006.

[7] Rau´ l Fidalgo-Merino and Marlon Nu´n˜ez, —Self-Adaptive Induction of Regression Trees IEEE transactions on pattern analysis and machine intelligence, vol. 33, no. 8, august 2011.

[8] Rodrigo Coelho Barros, M´arcio Porto Basgalupp, Andr´e C. P. L. F. de Carvalho, and Alex A. Freitas,‖ A Survey of Evolutionary Algorithms for Decision-Tree Induction‖ IEEE transactions on systems, man, and cybernetics—part c: applications and reviews, vol. 42, no. 3, may 2012.

[9]H. Zhao, —A multi-objective genetic programming approach to developing Pareto optimal decision trees,‖ Decision Support Syst., vol. 43, no. 3, pp. 809–826, 2007.

[10] Nathan Eagle, PhD,‖ The Reality Mining Data README,‖ Massachusetts Institute of Technology.

[11] J.Han, M.Kamber (2001) "Data Mining: Concepts and Techniques", Morgan Kaufmann Publishers, San Francisco.

[12] Wikipedia (2001), "Reality Mining" available at http://en.wikipedia.org/wiki/Data_mining (14-AUG-2012).

[13] Nathan Eagle, Alex Pentland, and David Lazer (2009), "Inferring Social Network Structure using Mobile Phone Data" In Proc. of the National Academy of Sciences (PNAS). Vol 106 (36), Clark University, Worcester, MA, pp.15274-15278.

[14] Wikipedia, (2001) Reality Mining, available at http://en.wikipedia.org/wiki/Reality_mining (6-OCT-2012).

[15] J.Han and M.Kamber (2000) "Data Mining Concepts and techniques", Morgan Kaufmann, San Francisco.

[16] RDatamining, R software detail, available at http://www.rdatamining.com/package.

[17] The R Project for Statistical Computing, R software available at http://www.r-project.org/.

www.ingramcontent.com/pod-product-compliance
Lightning Source LLC
Chambersburg PA
CBHW051213050326
40689CB00008B/1298

* 9 7 8 3 6 5 9 5 1 6 2 7 6 *